30-DAY DEVOTIONAL

Beautifully ABLE

LYNN THOMPSON

Copyright © 2025 Lynn Thompson

All rights reserved. No part of this publication may be reproduced, distributed, or transmitted in any form or by any means, including photocopying, recording, or other electronic or mechanical methods, without the prior written permission of the publisher, except in the case of brief quotations embodied in critical reviews and certain other noncommercial uses permitted by copyright law. For permission requests, write to the publisher, addressed "Attention: Permissions Coordinator," at the email address below.

Paperback: 978-1-951475-38-3

First paperback edition: February 2025

All Scripture quotations, unless otherwise indicated, are taken from the Holy Bible, New International Version®, NIV®.

Copyright ©1973, 1978, 1984, 2011 by Biblica, Inc.™ Used by permission of Zondervan. All rights reserved worldwide. www.zondervan.com. The "NIV" and "New International Version" are trademarks registered in the United States Patent and Trademark Office by Biblica, Inc.™

Scripture quotations marked NKJV are taken from the New King James Version®. Copyright © 1982 by Thomas Nelson. Used by permission. All rights reserved.

Scripture quotations marked (ESV) are from The ESV® Bible (The Holy Bible, English Standard Version®), © 2001 by Crossway, a publishing ministry of Good News Publishers. Used by

permission. All rights reserved.

Scripture quotations marked (KJV) are from the King James Version, Public Domain

Arrow Press Publishing
Summerville, SC 29486
www.arrowpresspublishing.com

Contents

Ackowledgements 5
Introduction 7

1. Boundary Lines 9
2. Alignment 13
3. An Anointing of Your Own 17
4. Action Words 21
5. Connecting with God 25
6. Destroy the Sin 29
7. Do Something! 35
8. Don't Get Comfortable 39
9. Dormancy 43
10. Every Word 47
11. Gaining Ground 51
12. Iron Sharpens Iron 55
13. Prayers of the Generations 59
14. Lead by Love, Grace & Truth 63
15. Why Worship Is So Important 67
16. God Gave Us Promises 71

17. Provisions	75
18. Dry Bones	79
19. Exchanging Your Burdens	83
20. Are You Smarter Today?	87
21. Stop Striving—My Grace is Sufficient	91
22. Weapons of Mass Destruction	95
23. God Makes Good from What Satan Intends for Evil	101
24. Contender	105
25. The Right Tools	111
26. Representatives of Christ	115
27. God's Will	119
28. Reconciliation	123
29. Unnecessary Battles	127
30. Trading Up	131

Acknowledgements

First, I want to thank God for meeting me, talking with me, teaching me, and directing me in the pathway that He has for me and allowing me to do things that I would have never dreamed I could do. Thank you, God.

Then I want to thank my husband for encouraging me and trusting my relationship with God to say yes when God speaks and allowing me the time to do what God speaks for me to do. I want to thank our two beautiful daughters, Megan and Mirssia, who have tolerated all my stories and ramblings over the many years, as mothers sometimes do. As I tried to put together what I thought God was saying to me and they had to be my first audience. Thank you, girls.

To our wonderful sons-in-law, Joe and Scotty, thank you for your support and love of our girls, the kids, and our family always. To Lena Gilley, my sweet friend, who encourages me and has always taught me to see beyond what I see with the natural eye. To my publisher, Tim Twigg, you are amazing with your ability to encourage me to believe that I can do all things through Christ, who gives me strength even when I know my shortcomings.

Most of all, this book is dedicated to our grandchildren so that they will always know that God speaks and they will be able to pass stories down from generation to generation. So, to my Ivan, Ellie Mae, Lainey Jo, Liam Scott, Mason, and Allie, this is for you and your children, many years to come. I love you all so much.

Introduction

Why the cover picture? I love nature! God speaks to me in nature. John 17:16-19 says, "They do not belong to this world any more than I do. Make them holy by your truth; teach them your word, which is truth. Just as you sent me into the world, I am sending them into the world. And I give myself as a holy sacrifice for them so they can be made holy by your truth."

The Mangrove trees are in this world, even though their conditions of living in brackish or extremely salty water are toxic, and they shouldn't survive, and most trees would not be the same as us. We are living in a fallen world that is so toxic, and we are attempting to survive as different circumstances surround us, and we have to reach for something or someone to help direct, guide, assist, or heal us to the pathway that puts things back in order for us.

I couldn't help but think of the Mangrove Trees that I got the opportunity to kayak through in Key West many years ago. Mangrove trees adjust with the waves, and the highs and lows of the tides do not wash them away because of their special root systems. They thrive in conditions and surroundings that most trees could not survive, such as the saltiness of the water or low oxygen, yet here they are thriving and providing shelter for marine life of all kinds. The trees are so beautiful and shouldn't be able to survive in these harsh conditions, but they do. Just like the mangrove tree, you are beautifully able to overcome your circumstances when you are anchored together as an intricate root system in the love of Jesus Christ.

DAY 1

Boundary Lines

"But don't be afraid of those who threaten you. For the time is coming when everything that is covered will be revealed, and all that is secret will be made known to all."

MATTHEW 10:26

I love how the Word of God is sometimes so complex yet simple. God intended it to be comprehensible to all who wish to understand. When revelation occurs, we recognize God's presence in everything around us. What we experience daily often reminds us of the examples and parables in Scripture.

BEAUTIFULLY ABLE

Every home has defined property lines. These lines communicate where your possession begins and ends. When someone crosses that line, they are on your property, and if they have come uninvited, they are trespassing. They have chosen to cross the boundary lines without permission.

One morning, while preparing for my day, with much to do and no time for error to make every appointment happen, I got in my vehicle and pulled down the driveway. I stopped at the end of the drive to look both ways before pulling out onto the road when suddenly I spotted something entirely unexpected. A multi-brown colored snake lay smashed on the road and eaten by birds. Seeing the snake at the boundary line of my property, my first thought was, you can't cross the bloodline—and you can't cross my property line either, just like the protection lines drawn around our lives of God's protection. And just as the snake couldn't cross, neither can the enemy. The enemy intends to get as close as possible to intimidate, frustrate, and wear us out; as near as this snake got to my property, that snake did not cross onto my land. My property line began right where the pavement and concrete meet, and although I didn't have to go out and kill the snake, it was dead right on the other side of my property line, and birds were cleaning it up for me. Thank you, Jesus!

Jesus fights for us. Why does He fight for us? We are in a covenant with Jesus Christ, and part of this unbreakable covenant is that His blood protects against enemy schemes.

"But the blood on your doorposts will serve as a sign, marking the houses where you are staying. When I see the blood, I will pass over you. This plague of death will not touch you when I strike the land of Egypt."
EXODUS 12:13-28

Now, the snake was a snake. It was not the devil and probably did not have the devil in it. Still, God allowed me to see this simple reminder of Scripture, and I'm grateful for the blood of Christ that has been applied to my family's life. We are continually reminded that Satan cannot cross the bloodline.

Ask God to reveal what boundary lines and protections he has provided for you, and thank him. However, also ask God to reveal to you what boundary lines you have allowed to cross.

What boundary lines do you need to enforce in your life?

REFLECT

DAY 2

Alignment

Don't worry about anything; instead, pray about everything. Tell God what you need and thank him for all he has done. Then, you will experience God's peace, which exceeds anything we can understand. His peace will guard your hearts and minds as you live in Christ Jesus. And now, dear brothers and sisters, one final thing. Fix your thoughts on what is true and honorable, and right, and pure, and lovely, and admirable. Think about things that are excellent and worthy of praise. Keep putting into practice all you learned and received from me—everything you heard from me and saw me doing. Then the God of peace will be with you.

PHILIPPIANS 4:6-9

When God speaks a direction or word of knowledge into your life, he is revealing to you that there is a plan, and he allows us the freedom to make the choices, and through prayer, we choose the right Master's plan. When things get confusing it will seem as though there is no good plan for you or too many directions to go but there will always be a way that seems right or easy and a way that is right but it just may not happen exactly as quickly as we would like or the way we may want it to happen. God has a plan to align your thoughts and your vision with his. God will always accomplish what he speaks, so when you hear different voices that seem to sound as if you are questioning yourself in an accusatory way, or even questioning God. Satan will attempt to confuse you so that he can crowd out the voice of God. He does not want you to compare your thoughts with what God says about you or for you.

What are some of the voices that you might hear that are trying to misalign your steps? They might sound something like, God isn't listening to my prayers, God doesn't care about my situation, Is God real, or the big one...Did God REALLY say that? When you start to hear these destructive questions going off in your head, stop and let God know that something has got you out of balance with what he has said to you or has said in His Word. The Word is always our magnifying glass. It will illuminate the truth and help redirect our steps to the path God has for us.

Take time for prayer. Prayer is how we connect with God. Through prayer, we can pull down the lies or accusations from the enemy and filter them through the lens of Scripture so that we will know what is true or not. Remember, stay aligned with the Word of God. Keep reading His Word, connecting with God, and praying because God's Word tells us in Psalms 34:18 that the LORD is close to the broken-hearted; he rescues those whose spirits are crushed.

God cares about what you care about. Like a good Father, he insists, "Keep on asking, and you will receive what you ask for. Keep on seeking, and you will find. Keep on knocking, and the door will be opened to you." (Matthew 7:7)

Align yourself with what God is saying, or you will be swept away by every deceptive doctrine by thinking it is a move of God. No, His Word does not change. Be anchored and aligned with what He is saying because His Word does not change. As we align with God's will, we also receive His anointing, which equips us to do the work He has called us to.

> *And you will hear of wars and threats of wars, but don't panic. Yes, these things must occur, but the end won't follow immediately. Nations will go to war against nation, and kingdom against kingdom. There will be famines and earthquakes in many parts of the world.*
>
> **MATTHEW 24:6-7**

When we align ourselves with God's truth, we are better prepared to face challenges with His strength and wisdom.

What negative words or fears have you been dealing with that you need to bring back in alignment with the Word of God?

REFLECT

DAY
3

An Anointing of Your Own

Taste and see that the LORD is good. Oh, the joys of those who take refuge in him!

PSALM 34:8

You may have heard someone say that a person is anointed, or they are "operating in their anointing". But what does the word "anointing" even mean? It means to be set apart or blessed by God.

King David declared, 'Taste and see that the Lord is good.' We experience God's goodness and anointing when we step into His calling for us. God sovereignly puts people in places. God has placed a unique anointing on each of us. It's not something we earn or create—it's a gift given to fulfill His unique purpose in our lives. You haven't arrived by your own strength, so you don't need to rely on your strength to take you where the Lord calls you.

Your anointing is far-reaching, even into places you cannot see. A good tree produces good fruit, while a bad tree does not produce good fruit. The Lord is not double-minded; therefore, the good and evil spirits will not cohabitate. Sin flees when in the presence of the living God of Israel.

You may not always see your anointing because it is not of you. It is of God, and what He does is far-reaching. Many eat of your fruit that you may never know; they reap blessings from your obedience. Here is an example from a friend's life.

My friend heard from God that they should open a gym and help rebuild people—to help build their confidence. But the gym industry can often be rude and prideful. My friend and her husband said, "Yes, Lord, you can trust us to lift your standard in what can be a dark place." They opened a gym, and she now provides individual guidance through personal training and physical therapy for people who have sustained injuries. When my friend and her husband said, 'Yes, Lord,' they didn't realize how far-reaching their obedience would be. But through their anointing, lives were and are being transformed, not only in the gym but in the homes of those they served."

The client who gets this guidance then shares it with family members and friends who benefit from the one who attends the training and physical therapy. These people also receive wisdom, which may seem unfair, but it is God's wisdom and anointing. He rewards and blesses abundantly. The wisdom that comes from the Lord should not be withheld. God's truth creates a ripple effect like a rock thrown into a still pond. The gym owners see the improvements of the client they are pouring into and possibly those close to that person. They often don't see beyond that, but God is still working, ripple after ripple, as their clients share the good news of healing and regained strength.

Similarly, we go into the house of the Lord, our community, and our workspaces and serve. As you do this, your loving kindness is far-reaching beyond what you can see. God is sending your individual gifts home with the people you meet, and they pour out into their families and friends. Let your fruit be sweet as the love of God is spreading. What unique anointing has God placed on your life? Seek His guidance today and ask Him to show you how to walk in it, for His glory."

REFLECT

DAY 4

Action Words

So, encourage each other and build each other up, just as you are already doing.

1 THESSALONIANS 5:11

These older women must train the younger women to love their husbands and their children, to live wisely and be pure, to work in their homes, to do good, and to be submissive to their husbands. Then they will not bring shame on the Word of God. In the same way, encourage the young men to live wisely. And you yourself must be an example to them by doing good works of every kind. Let everything you do reflect the integrity and seriousness of your teaching. Teach the truth so that your teaching can't be criticized. Then those who oppose us will be ashamed and have nothing bad to say about us.

TITUS 2:3-5

BEAUTIFULLY ABLE

Our words have the power to shape the lives of those around us. But words alone aren't enough—action brings our faith to life.

Have you ever had one of those moments when you see something—that has always been there—for the first time? This happened to me last week when I walked in my back door and looked up at a picture that's been hanging in the same place for at least ten years. I've loved the inscription and have read it for years, but recently, when I read it, I froze. The words on my picture are:

Deep ties, Express love, Hug each other, Never give up

As I looked at this picture, which had hung in my home for years, its words suddenly stood out to me uniquely: 'Express love, hug each other, never give up.' These words aren't just for decoration—they're actions we live by. Cherished memories and indelible moments flooded my mind and took me to special times when Dad would tell us that "family sticks together, no matter what." The moments of fellowship over family dinners or football games stood out to me. These words have described the relationship between my parents, siblings, and me, and we have passed them down to our children to make our home and family a haven for each other.

I took a minute and evaluated how much each one of these words described my life. I compared various areas of my life to these words. At times, I could see places where I had failed but could also rejoice in the areas where I was doing well. I realized that family is a more significant word than mom, dad, brothers, sisters, children, and grandchildren. There are people in our lives who also become family by a connection of the heart. We see some people every week, some a few times a year, and others only occasionally. The love remains no matter what. Take time for family before time passes you by because time doesn't slow down for anyone.

My goal for this year is not to be in the best shape of my life so that I can wear jeans without elastic, to eat all organic for better health, to travel every month of the year, or to read every book I would like to, although those things are important and do make me a better person for my family and friends. I will be doing some of them, but my goal will be to work on these action words by encouraging, building up, and spending time with people, training those younger than me, and making relationships count for the kingdom.

Let's not just talk about love, kindness, and encouragement—let's live it out daily. This week, find one way to put your faith into action: express gratitude, love, and encouragement to your family or friends. Perhaps it will be a kind note or a hard conversation where you ask for forgiveness (or forgive someone else). Either way, it's time to engage your faith through action steps. What better way to start than with the people who are closest to you?

REFLECT

DAY 5

Connecting with God

But Moses replied, "Are you jealous for my sake? I wish all the LORD'S people were prophets and the LORD would put his Spirit upon them all!"

NUMBERS 11:29

The most important relationship you can ever have is your connection with God. Moses understood this, and his deep connection with God brought freedom to an entire nation. Moses' obedience to God's voice brought about the end of slavery for Israel, restored their identity, returned their wealth, established their religion, and predicted their promised land.

But Moses realized that he needed help in doing so. In Numbers 11:29, he comes to the revelation of the Lord that the answer to his problems is that all people need a relationship with God—a relationship that is their very own.

Moses's relationship with God gave him wisdom, understanding, and direction from the Spirit. He knew of the divine possibilities that come with the presence and voice of God. Having their own relationship with God would allow the people to seek answers and miracles for their problems and not require Moses to provide for them. They could be comforted, guided, emotionally and spiritually developed, and, best of all, self-governed. What a revelation! What a possibility! He wanted them to connect with God. Like Moses, we sometimes wish that everyone could experience the same close relationship with God. But it's up to each of us to seek Him and develop our connection that can guide us through life's challenges."

But the people only saw Moses and not God. In Exodus 20:19, they tell him, "Speak to us yourself and we will listen. But do not have God speak to us or we will die."

We must not be like the Israelites who depended on someone else's relationship with God to guide them. We must diligently seek the Lord for ourselves.

God's guidance, direction, and discipline will always move us into a right relationship with Him. We help in this process by making ourselves available to Him.

Today's technological advancements can keep us distracted from God. Technology is good and a gift from God, but by placing appropriate limitations on it, we keep ourselves from being too busy to seek God for ourselves. Getting a word here and there, grabbing a Scripture out of context and trying to use it as a bandage, and then hoping it will fix the problem is not how God wants us to do things. Put aside anything that takes you away from hearing God for yourself. He wants to talk with you directly. He is available and has done His part to make sure there will never be anything from Him that will separate you from the knowledge of Him.

> *And I am convinced that nothing can ever separate us from God's love. Neither death nor life, neither angels nor demons, neither our fears for today nor our worries about tomorrow—not even the powers of hell can separate us from God's love. No power in the sky above or on the earth below—indeed, nothing in all creation will ever be able to separate us from the love of God that is revealed in Christ Jesus our Lord.*
>
> **ROMANS 8:38-39**

Can anything ever separate us from Christ's love? Does this mean He no longer loves us if we have trouble or calamity—or are persecuted, or hungry, or destitute, or in danger, or threatened with death? (Psalm 44:22 tells us, "For your sake we are killed every day; we are being slaughtered like sheep"). No, despite all these things, overwhelming victory is ours through Christ who loved us. Don't rely on someone else's relationship with God to guide you. Spend time today in prayer, seeking His voice for yourself."

REFLECT

Destroy the Sin

One day Samuel said to Saul, "It was the LORD who told me to anoint you as king of his people, Israel. Now listen to this message from the LORD! This is what the LORD of Heaven's Armies has declared: I have decided to settle accounts with the nation of Amalek for opposing Israel when they came from Egypt. Now go and completely destroy the entire Amalekite nation—men, women, children, babies, cattle, sheep, goats, camels, and donkeys."

1 SAMUEL 15:1-3

God doesn't just ask for our sacrifice—He demands our obedience. When we obey, we align ourselves with His will and receive His blessings. Saul thought he knew better than God, and that pride cost him everything. God's heart broke when He had to remove His anointing from Saul. God gave a command, a plan, a strategy to destroy the sin and leave no residue. But Saul did not follow through. He chose the pride of life by bringing the king back, which showed strength to the people during this time. He chose the best of the sheep and goats, the cattle, the fat calves, and the lambs—everything that appealed to them. They destroyed what was worthless or of poor quality. Saul defeated the Amalekites and was going to offer the loot of cattle to the Lord, but God wanted obedience, not sacrifice.

> *What shall I give you?" he asked. "Don't give me anything," Jacob replied. "But if you will do this one thing for me, I will go on tending your flocks and watching over them: Let me go through all your flocks today and remove from them every speckled or spotted sheep, every dark-colored lamb and every spotted or speckled goat. They will be my wages. And my honesty will testify for me in the future, whenever you check on the wages you have paid me. Any goat in my possession that is not speckled or spotted, or any lamb that is not dark-colored, will be considered stolen.*

GENESIS 30:31-33

Victorious kings would bring back the kings they defeated and imprison them or kill them as a witness to the people that they had been protected, and this enemy was no longer against them. Saul brought back King Agag for his ego and did not kill him or defeat his enemy, which made the people uneasy because the enemy was still alive.

We can be like that when we go through trials and need God to fight our battles. He has a plan and gives instructions, and we are to obey His plan of success. But sometimes, we remove the parts we don't like but keep the sins we are not ready to give up. Or we may think these are the things God has granted, and we can add to what God is doing. Make no mistake: God does not need our help; we need His help. Because Saul did this, God rejected him and regretted ever making him king.

Pride had taken root, and God had Samuel tell Saul that God had departed from him. Samuel found Saul in Carmel, setting up a monument to himself. When Saul saw Samuel coming, he greeted him cheerfully, utterly unaware that God had rescinded His anointing because Saul was so focused on himself.

After being confronted, Saul asked for forgiveness, but then he wanted to go on as usual, not to mention destroying the loot. Likewise, when we sin, how many times do we go on thinking, That's okay. It doesn't matter. There is always a difference between what God provides and what we do in our own strength. Remember the difference in how Jacob's herd was identified from his father-in-law's? God creates a difference in obedience and a heart to do the right thing.

The seed of jealousy and revenge grew in the heart of Saul when Samuel said, "The LORD has torn the kingdom of Israel from you today and has given it to someone else—one who is better than you" (1 Samuel 15:28). Can you imagine being such a leader and hearing that you have been replaced by someone more significant than you? That would hurt. Then Samuel had King Agag brought to him to destroy him, as he knew it was obedience to the Lord. May we be obedient to the Lord as Samuel was.

Are there areas in your life where you've held back from complete obedience? Ask God to reveal those areas and give you the strength to follow His plan.

REFLECT

DAY
7

Do Something!

The Spirit of the Lord is upon me, for he has anointed me to bring Good News to the poor. He has sent me to proclaim that captives will be released, that the blind will see, that the oppressed will be set free.

LUKE 4:18

We often wonder what our purpose is. People usually have different ideas when they talk about discovering their purpose. Some ask what job they should hold, what entrepreneurial adventure they should embark on, who they should marry, or what God is asking them to do from the eternal perspective. The answer can be as simple as serving others and bringing them the Good News of Christ, or it could be rather complex, wherein the answer to the question comes after a series of faith steps and acts of obedience.

Whether you choose to marry or remain single, take a job, or change careers, remember that your greater Kingdom purpose remains the same—to share Christ's love wherever you go. And although your questions are important, you can't lose sight of what really matters in the end. People won't be comparing salaries or job titles in heaven. They'll see legacy and eternal impact.

Our focus becomes much clearer when we realize that God allows us to make choices. Do you want to be married, and does it line up? If so, get married and take Good News to the poor, proclaim that captives will be released, that the blind will see, that the oppressed will be set free. Do you want to know what job to take? Take a job, then bring Good News to the poor; proclaim that captives will be released, that the blind will see, that the oppressed will be set free.

God gives us purpose here on earth, which comes from our relationship with Him and abiding in His presence. We must take steps in life and not just sit back and fold our arms and say, "Here I am, God, use me!"

God used Moses to deliver the Israelites from slavery. God told Moses that He was going to deliver them. God even told Moses the directions, and they led to the sea. That would initially seem frustrating, but if God's directions are correct, God would provide the way. Exodus 14:15-16, God said to Moses: "Why cry out to me? Speak to the Israelites. Order them to get moving. Hold your staff high and stretch your hand out over the sea; Split the sea! The Israelites will walk through the sea on dry ground. Don't wait for the perfect moment. Take the next step in faith, knowing that God has already given you a clear purpose.

Perhaps we should stop asking if our actions align with God's purpose for our lives and begin seeking to understand how we can instill God's purpose in all we do. It doesn't matter how mundane the element is; you can do it as unto the Lord.

> *Whatever you do, work at it with all your heart, as working for the Lord, not for human masters, since you know that you will receive an inheritance from the Lord as a reward. It is the Lord Christ you are serving.*
> **COLOSSIANS 3:23-24**

Don't get overwhelmed by big actions. What small steps can you take toward doing something significant?

REFLECT

Don't Get Comfortable

But I have this complaint against you. You don't love me or each other as you did at first! Look how far you have fallen! Turn back to me and do the works you did at first. If you don't repent, I will come and remove your lampstand from its place among the churches.

REVELATION 2:4-5

Have you gotten too comfortable in your faith? Has your waiting period made things familiar, and although you know it isn't right, have you settled into the present situation and are no longer doing the work it takes to stand? It's easy to settle into a routine and lose the passion we once had.

BEAUTIFULLY ABLE

If you've ever played the children's game *Pin the Tale on the Donkey*, you'll know what makes it hard is being blindfolded and spun around repeatedly until you are off balance and have lost your sense of direction. Sometimes, it takes a minute to steady yourself and stand still, but even in doing so, you may find yourself pointing in the wrong direction.

The enemy consistently strives to pull us off balance and point us in the wrong direction. He desires to blind us to the spiritual battles around us and keep us comfortable in our apathy.

Are you just a little off balance? You can't explain why you feel off and are unsure what to do to feel normal again. You should be doing better than you are, but you can't seem to get it together. Or are you in the flow but can't press in all the way? Don't let your love for God grow cold. Today, recommit yourself to standing firm in His presence and passionately pursuing Him.

Are you trying to resurrect dead things? Let go! Let God breathe into your situation so that life can come into it. You have been working on the wrong things. Be still and stand. Put on your armor and stand. As Psalm 46:10 says, "Be still and know that I am God! I will be honored by every nation. I will be honored throughout the world."

Consider Ephesians 6:13–18 from The Message:

> *Be prepared. You're up against far more than you can handle on your own. Take all the help you can get, every weapon God has issued, so you'll still be on your feet when it's all over but the shouting. Truth,*

righteousness, peace, faith, and salvation are more than words. Learn how to apply them. You'll need them throughout your life. God's Word is an indispensable weapon.

In the same way, prayer is essential in this ongoing warfare. Pray hard and long. Pray for your brothers and sisters. Keep your eyes open. Keep each other's spirits up so no one falls behind or drops out. Remember, God hasn't given up on you. He's waiting with open arms, ready to reignite your love for Him.

Perhaps you feel unsteady because God is pulling you out of comfort so that you can grow. In those growing seasons, it may feel like you are trying to get your footing right like you are trying to find a firm foundation again. Don't succumb to the temptation to return to who you used to be. Get comfortable being uncomfortable, and you'll see God use you in ways you never thought possible.

REFLECT

Dormancy

Then, turning to his disciples, Jesus said, "That is why I tell you not to worry about everyday life—whether you have enough food to eat or enough clothes to wear. For life is more than food, and your body more than clothing. Look at the ravens. They don't plant or harvest or store food in barns, for God feeds them. And you are far more valuable to him than any birds! Can all your worries add a single moment to your life? And if worry can't accomplish something like that, what's the use of worrying over bigger things? Look at the lilies and how they grow. They don't work or make their clothing, yet Solomon in all his glory was not dressed as beautifully as they are. And if God cares so wonderfully for flowers that are here today and thrown into the fire tomorrow, he will certainly care for you. Why do you have so little faith? And don't be concerned about what to eat and what to drink. Don't worry about such things. These things dominate

BEAUTIFULLY ABLE

the thoughts of unbelievers all over the world, but your Father already knows your needs. Seek the Kingdom of God above all else, and he will give you everything you need."

LUKE 12:22-31

Going down the interstate, as I listened to the Word of God and looked at the trees along the road, I thought, Wow. Trees have always been here. They're so beautiful, and they know the season they are in. Nobody must tell them what to do. They just know because God spoke it into them. In times of dormancy, we're not stagnant —we're growing deeper, laying the foundation for the next season of fruitfulness.

Just as trees have a season of growth and dormancy so that they can be refreshed and go a little deeper with their roots because if they don't, they will not be able to handle the next season's beauty, our spiritual lives also have seasons of rest and renewal.

God already knew everything they would need to do and supplied them with what they would need. Likewise, He knew what we would need and supplied it. He knew that we would need oxygen and provided it. Even before there was an interstate or vehicle, He knew that we would need sound buffers and provided us with all these trees that provide so much more than we can ever imagine. Some trees provide shade, some produce fruit, and some produce nuts. He knew all of this the first week of existence and called everything in that tree forth when He created it.

So, what has God put in you from the beginning so that others are blessed when it springs forth? He knows the plans He has for you and has equipped you for every good work so you will succeed when you operate in what He has anointed you to do. Humans were fashioned and designed to bless and help others as the trees do. He provides the miracles, and we must manage our seasons for the refueling.

> *For you created my inmost being you knit me together in my mother's womb. I praise you because I am fearfully and wonderfully made.*
> **PSALM 139:13-14 NIV**

Are you in a season of dormancy or growth? Trust that God is working in every season, preparing you for what's to come.

REFLECT

DAY 10

Every Word

But Jesus told him, "No! The Scriptures say, 'People do not live by bread alone, but by every word that comes from the mouth of God.'"

MATTHEW 4:4

———————

The Bible is a tool for living a godly life. We cannot pick and choose which verses to live by—we need all of God's truth to guide us. God reveals certain scriptures at certain times to encourage you and encourage others. When God gives you a Scripture, take time to meditate on it. Perhaps they are scriptures to live by, like the following:

BEAUTIFULLY ABLE

- Josiah who read the Word of God for the first time and it brought him to repentance and caused him to gather the people of Judah for the hearing of the Word and they began repairing the temple (2 Kings 23:1-30).

- The Proverbs 31 Woman who spoke wisely to her son to give advice on the ways of the priesthood, because we are chosen to be a royal priesthood (Proverbs 31:1-9).

- Ruth who found her kinsman-redeemer (Ruth 4:1-10); and

- Peter and John who gave what they had instead of silver and gold (Acts 3:6).

Meditating on the scriptures will encourage you, and you may realize *it's not just one passage you can live by. Every one of them makes up the Proverbs 31 woman (from Genesis to Revelation) or Ruth or the Good Samaritan. It takes every Word of God to make that virtue or character complete. We often think of specific scriptures that speak to us in certain moments. But living for Christ means applying every Word from the Bible, not just our favorite verses.*

We need Philippians 4:8 to know how to focus and how to think: "And now, dear brothers and sisters, one final thing. Fix your thoughts on what is true, and honorable, and right, and pure, and lovely, and admirable. Think about things that are excellent and worthy of praise."

We need 1 Thessalonians 5:11 to encourage us when we see someone struggling, to lift them up and not tear them down for trying to do something. "So, encourage each other and build each other up, just as you are already doing, to know how to speak to people."

We need Romans 1:28–32 for clear instructions on what to avoid to achieve the right way to live: "Since they thought it foolish to acknowledge God, he abandoned them to their foolish thinking and let them do things that should never be done. Their lives became full of every kind of wickedness, sin, greed, hate, envy, murder, quarreling, deception, malicious behavior, and gossip. They are backstabbers, haters of God, insolent, proud, and boastful. They invent new ways of sinning, and they disobey their parents. They refuse to understand, break their promises, are heartless, and have no mercy. They know God's justice requires that those who do these things deserve to die, yet they do them anyway. Worse yet, they encourage others to do them, too."

We need Revelation 22:18–19 as a reminder not to add to or take away from the Bible and to study all of the Bible instead of pulling out the parts we want to use.

We are to live by every Word that comes from the mouth of God. Make time this week to read through passages you don't usually focus on. Ask God to show you how His entire Word can shape your life.

REFLECT

DAY 11

Gaining Ground

I have given you every place where the sole of your foot will tread, just as I promised to Moses.

JOSHUA 1:3

God has given us the authority to take spiritual ground, but we must be ready to fight for it. It is by no mistake that I found a snake in our pool this morning. This was the second copperhead I have pulled out of the pool in the past three weeks. And he was angry. Why? Because either he would die or I would die. This one was a baby, but babies are more deadly because they have no control over the amount of venom in their bite, so their victim gets it all.

BEAUTIFULLY ABLE

I shuddered for a moment, then went to get my weapon to kill him as my daughter watched to make sure he didn't get out of the pool. It was either my family or him that would remain intact and alive. I had my weapon of choice—a hoe—stored in a back barn. I had to walk across the yard and through an area with possibly more snakes.

When I saw the snake in the pool, I knew it was more than a coincidence. It reminded me of our daily spiritual battles and the need to be vigilant. Putting this into a spiritual perspective, we must take authority over our territory of influence. Where I live, believers are taking new ground. People are attending classes to get free from addiction, and we have Holy Spirit–filled coordinators in place to help people with their walk as new believers; we have another set of coordinators to help disciple people in their walk with Christ, and we have more access at our local high school.

Satan and his minions are like the snakes in our pool. We must be constantly on guard and prepared to remove and dispatch them. We must never relax. Sometimes, we have a moment with God that is Holy Spirit-filled–and we think that will sustain us and the enemy will be afraid, so we holster our weapons. Know that the enemy never holsters his attacks. He is waiting for us to relax so he can try to cash in today on old events. We honor and remember times past when God has done great things, but we also must renew ourselves daily in the Word and the presence of God so that we can stand and fight and win. And to win, our weapons must be on us (our Bible) and in us (the Holy Spirit).

LYNN THOMPSON

Beware of Satan's snakes. Are you prepared to stand your ground? Keep your spiritual weapons ready—God has already given you the victory, but you must be prepared to fight.

REFLECT

DAY 12

Iron Sharpens Iron

As iron sharpens iron, so a friend sharpens a friend.

PROVERBS 27:17

Do you know what it takes to sharpen metal? It takes a stronger metal to sharpen softer metal. It's a metal that has already been through fire and has had the rough edges ground away.

We sharpen metals so they become functional in their intended state of being. We need one another to grow stronger in our walk with God. Just as iron sharpens iron, we sharpen each other through encouragement, accountability, and love. In the same way, we, as brothers and sisters in Christ who have been through the fires of life and are still standing, must sharpen the struggling ones who need refreshing and encouragement. At times, we all need to be reminded what God, the Creator, the One who is a Way Maker and made a plan for our life, says to and about us.

I've been through many tough times—some victories and some struggles. But through it all, I've learned that we grow best when we lift each other up, pointing one another back to God's truth. I have not arrived; I want to sharpen others, but not by saying, "I like your shirt," or "You look cute today." Although there is nothing wrong with that, and sometimes people need to hear that too, I want to sharpen others with something that will not wither away. Isaiah 40:8 says, "The grass withers and the flowers fade, but the Word of our God stands forever." So, I want to leave you with something that is forever true and cannot be taken away from you.

Are you in need of strength? Philippians 4:13 says, "I can do everything through Christ, who gives me strength." Seek God and see if He won't provide the strength you need for your situation. It is present, just there for the asking.

Are you feeling alone? Feeling like no one hears or understands what you are going through, and you are asking God for someone to just be present with you? Haggai 1:13 says, "Then Haggai, the LORD'S messenger, gave the people this message from the LORD:

'I am with you, says the LORD!'"

Are you dealing with health issues that have you in fear? Isaiah 41:10 says, "So do not fear, for I am with you; do not be dismayed, for I am your God. I will strengthen you and help you." And Deuteronomy 31:8 says, "It is the LORD who goes before you. He will be with you; he will not leave you or forsake you. Do not fear or be dismayed."

Are you in need of a financial breakthrough? Psalm 34:9–10 says, "Fear the LORD, you his holy people, for those who fear him lack nothing. The lions may grow weak and hungry, but those who seek the Lord lack no good thing."

Be sharpened by the truths that never change. Who can you encourage this week? Look for opportunities to sharpen others with God's Word, and surround yourself with those who can do the same for you.

REFLECT

DAY 13

Prayers of the Generations

Grass will grow and then it will wither; flowers will bloom and then they will die. But God's written message, the truth, will abide forever. All his promises will be fulfilled.

1 PETER 1:25

Prayer is a legacy we leave behind. The prayers of those who came before us bear fruit in our lives today and will shape future generations. In the Old Testament, when God's presence was so evident, and He accomplished impossible things, the Israelites would place a stone or stones in the place where it happened. These were their stones of remembrance and experiences never to be forgotten.

BEAUTIFULLY ABLE

I come from a family of prayer warriors. Though our family history is messy, I've been blessed by the prayers offered by generations before me. Their faithfulness has impacted my life in ways I'll never fully understand. In my family, generations before me have placed stones of remembrance in areas of opposition to the right path in our family's life. We hear it through the stories that we tell from generation to generation. My family is known to have many storytellers. If you spend any time with my relatives, you will hear stories. It takes time to tell a story, but time well spent builds relationships.

I come from a very messy family. You can name the worst and best of things; most of them are in my family. Still, as I sit here enjoying the little bit of coolness this morning on my back porch and listening to the sounds of wildlife all around me, I am aware that there has always been a remnant of prayer warriors in every generation of my family. Some are family members I have never met, and some still influence my life today. I am increasingly aware that the blessings in my life and the successes I experience are not just my own.

Our successes and blessings are due to the prayers and promises that have gone before us. Prayers do not die, nor do God's promises die. I know I am living out a God-promised life from someone who wrestled with God many years ago on different issues for my family and me and asked God to bless us. You may see one thing when you look at me and judge it as good or bad. You may judge from your standpoint however you want, but I understand I am drinking from good wells I did not dig.

Deuteronomy 6:10–12 puts it like this: "The LORD your God will soon bring you into the land he swore to give you when he made a vow to your ancestors Abraham, Isaac, and Jacob. It is a land with large, prosperous cities that you did not build. The houses will be richly stocked with goods you did not produce. You will draw water from cisterns you did not dig, and you will eat from vineyards and olive trees you did not plant. When you have eaten your fill in this land, be careful not to forget the LORD, who rescued you from slavery in the land of Egypt."

I am so very thankful for Jesus Christ and for the people in my life who have paved the way for me through prayer to make my life what it is today. Start building your prayer legacy today. Whether for your family, community, or future generations, your prayers will leave a lasting impact.

REFLECT

Lead by Love, Grace & Truth

The godly can look forward to a reward, while the wicked can expect only judgment.

PROVERBS 11:23

Christians are called to be examples of Christ's love and truth. Our lives should reflect His character so others are drawn to Him. New people are coming into the church, our workspaces, and our communities every day, and then there are some people we have known for a while and possibly grown up with. Things happen, and things are said that may cause them to be offended by God's Word when they are living in sin. It's not us that they don't like or snap back at—it is the Word in us. So don't take it personally, and remember, if they are not saved, they don't live by the same guidelines we do, so don't beat them up!

Proverbs 11:23 tells us that the godly look forward to the message—a sharpening, a prayer, an encouragement—and view it as a reward. How do we respond to a reward? With excitement and anticipation. I encourage you to keep the enthusiasm of God alive in your heart and mind, meditating on it daily so that the love of the Father is seen in you and through you.

Some in the body of Christ do not remain in the Word but still attend, partake, and connect with the body. However, some may find the Word to be judgmental or the body of Christ to be judgmental. It can be painful when people reject the truth, especially when it feels personal. But remember, they aren't rejecting you—they are struggling with the Word that convicts them. They will be critical. Critical of fellowship, critical of the message, and critical or cynical of the growth that is happening in the church.

Why do I bring this stern message? Be watchful for yourself in your conversations or what you entertain with others, especially with your teams. We are not to sound like the world. Lead by example in love, as Christ has loved you. Don't forsake your daily time with the Lord, and govern your walk with God. We can only give what we have to give away. Acts 3:6 says, "I don't have any silver or gold for you. But I'll give you what I have. In the name of Jesus Christ the Nazarene, get up and walk!"

Give what you have. Think about how you're living out your faith. Are you leading by example in love, grace, and truth? Look for ways to shine Christ's light in every situation.

REFLECT

DAY 15

Why Worship is So Important

He said, "Listen, all you people of Judah and Jerusalem! Listen, King Jehoshaphat! This is what the LORD says: Do not be afraid! Don't be discouraged by this mighty army, for the battle is not yours, but God's. Tomorrow, march out against them. You will find them coming up through the ascent of Ziz at the end of the valley that opens into the wilderness of Jeruel. But you will not even need to fight. Take your positions; then stand still and watch the LORD'S victory. He is with you, O people of Judah and Jerusalem. Do not be afraid or discouraged. Go out against them tomorrow, for the LORD is with you!"

Then King Jehoshaphat bowed low with his face to the ground. And all the people of Judah and Jerusalem did the same, worshiping the LORD. Then the Levites from the clans of Kohath and Korah stood to praise the LORD, the God of Israel, with a very loud shout.

BEAUTIFULLY ABLE

Early the next morning the army of Judah went out into the wilderness of Tekoa. On the way Jehoshaphat stopped and said, "Listen to me, all you people of Judah and Jerusalem! Believe in the LORD your God, and you will be able to stand firm. Believe in his prophets, and you will succeed."

After consulting the people, the king appointed singers to walk ahead of the army, singing to the LORD and praising him for his holy splendor. This is what they sang:

"Give thanks to the LORD; his faithful love endures forever!"

2 CHRONICLES 20:15-21

———————————

Worship isn't just about singing songs—it's a weapon that changes the spiritual atmosphere, bringing victory, peace, and clarity. When Jehoshaphat faced an overwhelming enemy, he didn't send out soldiers—he sent out worshippers. And as they praised God, the enemy destroyed itself. Worship changes everything. Your worship is incomparably important; it cuts through and exposes the sin in your life. Envy, strife, jealousy, anger, and rebellion of any kind are evil and come straight from the pit of hell. When you feel these things in the atmosphere or may be experiencing any of this, put on some scriptural worship. Worship in Spirit and truth. Worship is to God and about God, not you and your issues.

The Spirit of Christ and the Spirit of our old sinful flesh refuse and cannot dwell together. One has to leave! So worshipping in Spirit and truth clears the air of misconceptions, lies, anxiety, etc. These and other things do not want you to get the Word of God and Truth in you. The enemy does not want you equipped. He wants to steal or confuse the Word before you can digest it so you will not grow and help bring others into the kingdom. Matthew 13:3–9 says,

> *Listen! A farmer went out to plant some seeds. As he scattered them across his field, some seeds fell on a footpath, and the birds came and ate them. Other seeds fell on shallow soil with underlying rock. The seeds sprouted quickly because the soil was shallow. But the plants soon wilted under the hot sun, and since they didn't have deep roots, they died. Other seeds fell among thorns that grew up and choked out the tender plants. Still, other seeds fell on fertile soil, producing a crop that was thirty, sixty, and even a hundred times as much as had been planted! Anyone with ears to hear should listen and understand.*

Once saturated with God's presence, we can safely unsheathe our Weapon of Mass Destruction, the Word of God. The Word is preached and lands in fertile soil without those old buzzards' interference. Do you think those buzzards will try to return and place doubt in your mind? You better believe it; they will. But now you know how to fight against what comes against you. Worship like nobody is watching and see if the atmosphere doesn't change. Are you facing battles today? Turn on worship music and start praising God. Watch how the atmosphere shifts as you focus on Him.

REFLECT

DAY 16

God Gave Us Promises

Timothy, my son, I am giving you this command in keeping with the prophecies once made about you, so that by recalling them you may fight the battle well.

1 TIMOTHY 1:18 NIV

God's promises are for everyone. No matter your past, His promises stand firm, waiting for you to claim them. Paul, the writer of 1 Timothy, describes himself this way:

> *And I thank Christ Jesus our Lord who has enabled me, because He counted me faithful, putting me into the ministry, although I was for-*

BEAUTIFULLY ABLE

merly a blasphemer, a persecutor, and an insolent man; but I obtained mercy because I did it ignorantly in unbelief. And the grace of our Lord was exceedingly abundant, with faith and love which are in Christ Jesus. This is a faithful saying and worthy of all acceptance, that Christ Jesus came into the world to save sinners, of whom I am chief. However, for this reason I obtained mercy, that in me first Jesus Christ might show all long-suffering, as a pattern to those who are going to believe on Him for everlasting life. Now to the King eternal, immortal, invisible, to God who alone is wise, be honor and glory forever and ever. Amen.

1 TIMOTHY 1:12-17 NKJV

Paul had discipled Timothy and left him in leadership over the church at Ephesus. Very persuasive false teachers were attacking the gospel, and Timothy felt overwhelmed and somewhat over his head, or he was not even qualified in the matters he was facing. Like Timothy, we may come from broken places, but God's promises change everything. His promises give us a new future filled with hope.

Paul encourages Timothy to recall the promises of prophecies to give hope, direction, and confidence that God is for him. What do you think the promises were that he reflected on that you can apply today? Could it be that you need to be reminded, like Timothy, of God's promise to strengthen you, that He will not leave you, or even that He alone is your God? Sink yourself into the Truth of the Word and absorb what Isaiah says in verse 41:10, "So do not fear, for I am with you; do not be dismayed, for I am your God. I will strengthen and help you; I will uphold you with my righteous right hand."

Remember, Paul had overcome a shipwreck, was beaten with rods, and even stoned. How was it possible for Paul, Timothy, and us today to keep our minds on our Rescuer and Deliverer when the surroundings and experiences are so harsh? Paul was committed to truth and helping to spread that truth to those that he was discipling and all who would receive him. He tapped into Jeremiah 29:11, which says, "For I know the plans I have for you," says the Lord. They are plans for good and not for disaster, to give you a future and a hope.

The promises of God are available to us if we tap into them, no matter who we are or what we've done. Recall the promises of God, and when you know what God is saying, hold to it like Timothy had to do to remain steadfast in the truth to spread the gospel.

There are more than 3,500 promises in the Word of God, but I want to leave you with a small list of some quick reference ones that you can know right now:

1. God fights for us (Ex. 14:14, Deut 1:30, Isaiah 4:20)
2. God created us and knows us (Ps. 139)
3. God provides a way out of temptation (1 Cor. 10:13)
4. God gives us rest (Mat. 11:28)
5. God gives us eternal life (John 3:16-17)

Are you standing on God's promises today? Reflect on His promises in Scripture and claim them over your life.

REFLECT

DAY 17

Provisions

But Samuel replied, "What is more pleasing to the Lord: your burnt offerings and sacrifices or your obedience to his voice? Listen! Obedience is better than sacrifice, and submission is better than offering the fat of rams.

1 SAMUEL 15:22

No matter your situation, God has already provided the solution. His provision is always right on time. While reading my Bible this morning, I once again noticed a passage where God speaks something twice. When God says something twice, that means it is established.

BEAUTIFULLY ABLE

Genesis 41:32 says God gave the dream to Pharaoh in two forms. That's because God has firmly decided the matter. And it's because God will do it soon. This means you will go through the thing He has shown you. But God will give warnings, plans, instructions, and directions on what we should do when we seek him to know how to navigate what he shows us. This can be something good, or it could be a warning for us to get in our prayer time to get guidance through a situation like Joseph was able not just to explain the plans of God but also carry out the right plan to save people and a nation.

Then, there are times when He will only show or speak something to us once, and what does this mean? Can we change the mind of God?

Exodus 32:14 says, "When Moses heard this, he pleaded with God to turn from His anger. So, the Lord relented from the harm which He said He would do to His people." God allows us to partner with Him in prayer to turn a situation—not always, but sometimes. Sometimes, we must go through the problem to build our faith.

First Corinthians 10:13 tells us, "The temptations in your life are no different from what others experience. And God is faithful. He will not allow the temptation to be more than you can stand. When you are tempted, he will show you a way out so that you can endure." God always gives us a way out of something. The way out or through a situation is prayer. This does not mean you won't go through a trial or a tough time, but He will be with you and provide for you.

No matter what God has called you to, He provides for all your needs, to the tiniest details. Even if you fulfill all that God has called you to and it still doesn't work out how you thought it would, it is not on you. He provides all you need for obedience and is responsible for the results, not you.

Even in Jonah's disobedience, God provided for him—a plant to shade him, a second chance to fulfill his mission. God always provides what we need, even when we don't deserve it. Jonah 4:6 says, "And the LORD God arranged for a leafy plant to grow there, and soon it spread its broad leaves over Jonah's head, shading him from the sun. This eased his discomfort, and Jonah was very grateful for the plant." God set a plan in motion. He provided the transportation for Jonah to get where he needed to be. In the heat of a "heart battle," He even provided shade so that Jonah could complete the mission with obedience to the Lord.

Are you struggling to trust God's provision in your life? Rest in the knowledge that He sees your needs and is already working out the details.

REFLECT

DAY 18

Dry Bones

He asked me, "Son of man, can these bones live?"

EZEKIEL 37:3 NIV

When everything feels lost, God is the only one who can still bring life. He specializes in raising dead or dormant hopes, lost dreams, and dire situations. God is a jealous God. He will not let anyone profane His name, which is holy. What comes against you comes against God, and what comes against God will come against you. He will not allow you to remain feeling discouraged and feeling defeated.

God told Ezekiel to prophesy. Prophecy is speaking what God has said. I am so thankful that God has given us a Bible, a written form, to read and hear what He says. He is an encourager, and He speaks life to our dead situations.

I had never seen it before, as I did this time while reading about Ezekiel in the Valley of Dry Bones. How long must something be dead before the bones become dry, with no muscle, meat, or blood? It wasn't one thing that had died. Ezekiel said it was a valley of dry bones—plural. Sometimes hopes, dreams, and healings seem to get dashed again and again—and before you know it, one issue has laid up on another, and your intentions begin to defeat you because all you can recall when you look back is a valley of dry bones.

This is such an incredible example that we can understand. In the New Testament, we read that Jesus healed the immediate infirmities of some. Sometimes, Jesus healed a son or daughter who had just died. Then there was Lazarus, who died, and Jesus waited until the stink was on him—four days later—to bring him back to life. All so that we would believe. His words were, "Did I not tell you that if you believe, you will see the glory of God?" (John 11:40 NIV) Because the New Testament does not replace the Old Testament, they work hand in hand to show what God has done and what He still can do, and even greater is yet to come. Matthew 5:17, "Don't misunderstand why I have come. I did not come to abolish the law of Moses or the writings of the prophets. No, I came to accomplish their purpose.

What is your dire situation? Has it gone on so long that it is dead and dry and stinks?

Ezekiel was instructed to speak what he heard the Father say. In a New Testament example, Jesus was being tempted by Satan. Jesus did not get into a debate, try to reason with the temptation, or attempt to analyze what was happening. Jesus only spoke what the Father had already told him—and Satan had to flee (your fleshly desires and the Spirit of God cannot dwell together).

In Ezekiel's vision, a valley of dry bones came to life at God's command. No matter how dead your situation feels, God can breathe new life into it. So when God spoke to Ezekiel—to encourage him about who he was in a partnership with, to encourage him to believe again, to hope again—when God said prophesy to these bones, He was saying, "Let my Word breathe on this situation and what you see. Once life came upon those bones, what were they called? An army! An army that will serve Me and proclaim Me as Lord of lords and King of kings." This is the ultimate prodigal son or daughter story. This is the ultimate healing story. This is the ultimate story of how much God loves you—whether your need is immediate, four days late, or seems way past dead. His Words are still alive, and He gives breath and life to dead situations.

Do you feel like you're in a valley of dry bones? Ask God to breathe His life into your situation and watch as He works miracles. Let the Word of God get within your bones and begin to speak. I encourage you to seek what God says about your situation so you can call it to life.

REFLECT

DAY
19

Exchanging Your Burdens

Come to Me, all you who labor and are heavy laden, and I will give you rest. Take My yoke upon you and learn from Me, for I am gentle and lowly in heart, and you will find rest for your souls. For My yoke is easy and My burden is light.

MATTHEW 11:28-30 NKJV

The word "yoke" stood out in this passage because I lived on a farm and understood some of what this implies. When two animals on a farm are yoked together, it is as if they are wearing one set of reins with two bits so that they walk in step together to make the load lighter because two can pull more than one can. When two are yoked together, there is always one that is more experienced, equipped, and nurturing, and the leader will train the weaker or younger one if they only submit to the leadership. If the one learning will submit and walk in step with the leader, the weight is not as heavy, and the task at hand becomes balanced if it is shared. Also, different types of animals are never yoked together because they don't have the same attitudes, mindsets, or physical abilities.

> *Don't team up with those who are unbelievers. How can righteousness be a partner with wickedness? How can light live with darkness?*

2 CORINTHIANS 6;14

Jesus invites us to lay down our heavy burdens and take up His, which are light. This exchange brings peace, rest, and purpose. The key to getting rest is trading or exchanging your burdens for what burdens Christ. We're all carrying something—family issues, finances, or fear. But Jesus asks us to hand these over to Him. In return, He gives us His burden—a heart for the lost and the mission to share His love. With his burdens, we can walk in compassion, and we then have room in our hearts to be burdened with what burdens Christ's heart. He will take your burdens when you pick up His burden, which is salvation for the lost. Hell was never intended for us.

We are all born into the world and sentenced to death until we come to know Christ. If you have been set free, all heaven rejoices, but many have not yet been set free, and we must not forget about their eternity just because God has saved us. Ask God to give you

His heart and His burden for people. This is why some get up early on their day off and work passionately to set up an environment where the community can connect with the Word of God that cuts through the atmosphere of sin, brings them to deliverance, and saves their soul. We sharpen one another in fellowship. We were never meant to do life alone.

What burden are you carrying today? Give it to God in prayer and ask Him to replace it with His peace and purpose.

REFLECT

DAY 20

Are You Smarter Today?

As it is, there are many parts, but one body. The eye cannot say to the hand, "I don't need you!" And the head cannot say to the feet, "I don't need you!" On the contrary, those parts of the body that seem to be weaker are indispensable, and the parts that we think are less honorable we treat with special honor. And the parts that are unpresentable are treated with special modesty, while our presentable parts need no special treatment. But God has put the body together, giving greater honor to the parts that lacked it, so that there should be no division in the body. But that its parts should have equal concern for each other. If one part suffers, every part suffers with it; if one part is honored, every part rejoices with it.

1 CORINTHIANS 12:20-21

BEAUTIFULLY ABLE

At the end of each day, can you say that you're wiser, stronger, or more compassionate than you were the day before? Growth happens when we reflect on what God is teaching us. There is a funny little question my dad asks all the time: "Did you learn anything today? Are ya any smarter today than you were yesterday?" As I reflect on the tragic events of a church shooting at Mother Emanuel AME Church in our local area over the past twenty-four hours and all that God has allowed me to be a part of today with the visiting of the church and standing with hundreds of people that I do not know but singing hymns as a sign of mourning and celebration, I can say that I have learned something today. I have learned that love knows no boundaries, and I have realized more deeply how we are all connected in God's family."

In the past twenty-four hours, I have been speared with grief that has cut me to my soul. I don't even know the people who were attacked, but I know that they were a part of the body of Christ because I feel as if a piece of my heart has died. So, I do have a better understanding of this piece of the Word of God. I have no other explanation for my feelings than to say that this passage is true. As much pain and sorrow as I felt for the families and the church, I also felt joy and peace as a body of believers came together to understand that nothing can separate us from the love of God and that we are better together. So yes, Daddy, I learned something today and I do feel smarter.

LYNN THOMPSON

I am grateful for the cross and that I can serve God, who is the beginning and the end, the one true God. There has never been and will never be another God. He is the everlasting Father who makes our crooked ways straight; He is the I am, the One who was, the One that is, and the One to come. He holds my future days in His hands and makes perfect plans for my life, and I willingly give my life to Him to say, "It's yours. Do as you will with this life. And if you want to use this voice, this body, this energy to fulfill Your purposes, then I say, 'Let's roll.' Life is short, and everyone's life matters."

Take a moment today to reflect on how you've grown. Are you wiser, more loving, and more connected to others in the body of Christ than you were yesterday?

REFLECT

DAY 21

Stop Striving – My Grace is Sufficient

But suppose we seek to be made right with God through faith in Christ, and then we are found guilty because we have abandoned the law. Would that mean Christ has led us into sin? Absolutely not! Rather, I am a sinner if I rebuild the old system of law I already tore down. For when I tried to keep the law, it condemned me. So I died to the law—I stopped trying to meet all its requirements—so that I might live for God. My old self has been crucified with Christ. It is no longer I who live, but Christ lives in me. So I live in this earthly body by trusting in the Son of God, who loved me and gave himself for me. I do not treat the grace of God as meaningless. For if

BEAUTIFULLY ABLE

keeping the law could make us right with God, then there was no need for Christ to die.

GALATIANS 2:17-21

God never meant for us to live by a checklist of rules, trying to earn His approval. Instead, His grace frees us to live in the fullness of His love and mercy.

Grace means being approved and favored, given mercy, or pardoned. Second Corinthians 2:9 (NIV) tells us, "But he said to me, 'My grace is sufficient for you, for my power is made perfect in weakness.'" Some people are striving to live between this world and Christianity. The Word of God was never meant to tie us to the letter of the law. We should not be making a checklist and crossing T's and dotting I's with no joy or purpose. The commandments and laws were set to guide us to Christ, to direct us to Him, and to give us guardrails, but know that Jesus Christ was always the plan. He wasn't Plan B. He has always been the plan for your life, and His grace is sufficient.

Experiencing God's grace for myself, I prayed over a situation in my family until I literally could not pray anymore. I fasted. I prayed. "Just turn it over to God and let it go" was what I had heard so much in church, and I thought I was doing all the things I was supposed to be doing with no answer for three months. And then it happened; I pulled into my driveway after three months of almost nonstop praying, and I told God, "I can't do this anymore; if this situation happens the way I am asking for it not to, then so be it. I can't do anymore". That was the very moment that God stepped into my place, and where I lacked the right words, the right attitude, and the right heart, God filled me with His love and gave me the ability to go one more day to see His plan of redemption in my situation. It was more than I could have ever done on my own. His power is not pushy or arrogant but full of love and peace, and His peace is what rested in our home that day.

Are you trying to handle life in your own strength? Let go of the striving and ask God to fill you with His grace. He is ready to carry you through.

REFLECT

DAY 22

Weapons of Mass Destruction

And so, dear brothers and sisters, I plead with you to give your bodies to God because of all he has done for you. Let them be a living and holy sacrifice—the kind he will find acceptable. This is truly the way to worship him. Don't copy the behavior and customs of this world, but let God transform you into a new person by changing the way you think. Then, you will learn to know God's will for you, which is good, pleasing, and perfect.

Because of the privilege and authority God has given me, I give each of you this warning: Don't think you are better than you are. Be honest in evaluating yourselves, measuring yourselves by the faith God has given us. Just as our bodies have many parts and each part has a special function, so it is with Christ's body. We are many parts of one body and belong to each other.

God has given us different gifts for doing specific things well in his grace. So, if God has given you the ability to prophesy, speak out with as much faith as God has given you. If your gift is serving others, serve them well. If you are a teacher, teach well. If your gift is to encourage others, be encouraging. If it is giving, give generously. If God has given you leadership ability, take the responsibility seriously. And if you have a gift for showing kindness to others, do it gladly. Don't just pretend to love others. Love them. Hate what is wrong. Hold tightly to what is good. Love each other with genuine affection and take delight in honoring each other. Never be lazy, but work hard and serve the Lord enthusiastically. Rejoice in our confident hope. Be patient in trouble, and keep on praying. When God's people are in need, be ready to help them. Always be eager to practice hospitality. Bless those who persecute you. Don't curse them; pray that God will bless them. Be happy with those who are happy, and weep with those who weep. Live in harmony with each other. Don't be too proud to enjoy the company of ordinary people. And don't think you know it all! Never pay back evil with more evil. Do things in such a way that everyone can see you are honorable. Do all that you can to live in peace with everyone.

Dear friends, never take revenge. Leave that to the righteous anger of God. For the Scriptures say,

"I will take revenge;

I will pay them back,"

says the Lord.

Instead, "If your enemies are hungry, feed them.

If they are thirsty, give them something to drink.

In doing this, you will heap

burning coals of shame on their heads."

Don't let evil conquer you, but conquer evil by doing good

MATTHEW 11:28-30 NKJV

In spiritual warfare, we don't fight with physical weapons. Our most powerful weapon is the Word of God—our 'Weapon of Mass Destruction' against the enemy. This chapter is such a reset for not only our day, our work, and our language but also our minds. Be transformed in the mind with the precious words in this chapter. There is so much wisdom to help you succeed if you take heed of every anointed Word that drips from your Weapon of Mass Destruction pages—your Bible.

How do you live a life before people and before God that is honoring to the Lord? Verse 2 tells us not to copy the behavior and customs of this world. Verse 3 is direct, telling us not to think we are better than we are. We must evaluate ourselves honestly, measuring ourselves by the faith God has given us. Transformation begins in the mind. When we let God's Word renew our thoughts, we are better equipped to stand against the enemy's attacks.

Each one of us has been given gifts. That's right, gifts from God, the Holy One, the Lord of lords and King of kings. He has given us gifts to bring worship to Him. Everyone has something different; although some may be the same, they are provided to bring glory to the Father. Some may say, "I don't know what my gift is." What comes naturally and brings life to you and the body of Christ? Do you encourage, do you have the ability to give, do you show leadership? It's not because you have been put in that place but because God has established it in your DNA, and you can't escape it. Do you have a gift for showing kindness to others? Then, do what God has put within you and take the responsibility seriously.

Don't pretend to love others. People know love, and they know when love is not genuine. We only fool ourselves when the love of the Father is not within us. Serve with genuine affection and take delight in honoring each other. Hate what is wrong and hold tight to what is good. Don't be lazy, but work hard and serve the Lord enthusiastically. When people are in need, always be eager to practice hospitality. If it doesn't come naturally and you are living by faith to develop a spiritual muscle, practice it. For example, in our home, my husband Ray didn't pray out loud at first, and many years ago, we started with our meal prayers. We did not eat unless Ray prayed, and then his meal prayers became more and more developed, and his confidence grew, and that spiritual muscle was being defined and shaped to be able to pray for many needs—not just our food and our bodies.

Bless the ones that persecute you; pray blessings on them. For you are God's child, and if you have kids, you know what it is like for someone to speak ill against your child. Maybe this is only me, but I want to be completely transparent. This mother hen will zone in if you mess with my nest. LOL. So, I need this reminder to be constantly transformed in my mind to do what is right and to know that if I get that way, then doesn't God get that way about us, His children? It's not our responsibility to retaliate. We pray for them, and God will take care of things. Like a good parent, He has your back. Let's live in harmony with each other. Do all you can to live in peace with everyone. How do we do this? Verse 20 says that if your enemies are hungry, feed them. If they are thirsty, give them something to drink. Don't let evil conquer you, but conquer evil by doing good.

You are conquering evil through your work for the community and in your places of influence that God has entrusted you. Press in and press on, for we are in a precious time to be alive and do the kingdom's work.

Are you using God's Word as your primary weapon? Spend time each day reading Scripture and letting it transform your mind so that you can fight and win your spiritual battles.

REFLECT

God Makes Good from What Satan Intends for Evil

You intended to harm me, but God intended it all for good. He brought me to this position so I could save the lives of many people.

GENESIS 50:20

No matter how bad things look, God can turn what Satan meant for evil into something good. He's a master of redemption. Our Lord is the God who brings change and blessing. We all struggle with the flesh in one way or another, and we are all fighting battles within ourselves, but God is not struggling with it. He has already defeated it.

BEAUTIFULLY ABLE

We can consider the sins of our past and think, how could God ever use me? Or I have just done too much wrong. As I read through the Word, I keep seeing over and over again how God takes what Satan meant to be against God and His people and redeems it so that it looks completely new and makes it something that he can use for His good.

In 1 Chronicles 18:7–8, David brought the gold shields of Hadadezer's offers to Jerusalem and a large amount of bronze from Hadadezer's towns of Tebah and Cun. Later, Solomon melted the bronze and molded it into the great bronze basin called the sea, the pillars, and the various bronze articles used at the Temple. Originally, these items were used in the battle against King David and the Israelites, but once the towns were won, the very thing used to fight against them became repurposed in the blessings and dressings of the place where the Israelites worshipped.

King David's life was filled with battles. He fought anything that stood in his way from a very early age. He was offended at the thought of the Philistines making a fool of God's people, and he took up a cause to defend God's holy people and not only killed the giant but took his head off, too. He ran from his father-in-law, who had been jealous of him for a long time. He was able to retrieve the valuable metals from the various battles he had won in hopes that he would one day build a permanent house for the Lord. The metals were stored and kept in the hopes of a future place to worship the Lord. King David's son Solomon became king, and because David had battled for so long and so hard most of his life, God gave Solomon rest from battles, allowing him time to melt the bronze and mold it into the great bronze basin called the sea, the pillars, and the various bronze articles used at the Temple of God.

Are you facing a battle today? Trust that God is already working to redeem your situation, bringing something good from the struggle.

REFLECT

Contender

The Lord shall cause your enemies who rise up against you to be defeated before you; they will come out against you one way and will flee before you seven ways.

DEUTERONOMY 28:7

When you feel like you have lifted the same prayers repeatedly and you're not seeing anything happening, the truth is that someone lifts your prayers up even when you get weary and don't know how or what to pray anymore. God is your Contender!!

I was watching UFC fighting, and the announcer began describing the athletes coming up in the main event. He started by calling them contenders and describing their attitudes and accomplishments. The announcer said, "A contender will not rest until he conquers all in his way." I told my husband Ray, "Rewind that! I have to hear that again!" because my Spirit was listening to hear beyond what my ears could hear.

A contender will not rest until he conquers all in his way!

Do you know and believe that God hears your prayers? Not just because you pray that He hears you but because He promised to hear you and He is a promise keeper. Psalm 34:17 (NKJV) tells us, "The righteous cry out, and the LORD hears and delivers them out of all their troubles."

Scripture began to fill my mind, and I had to go on a search to see what God wanted to show me. I found David's prayer in Psalm 35:1–6 (ESV):

> *Contend, O Lord, with those who contend with me;*
>   *fight against those who fight against me!*
> *Take hold of shield and buckler*
>   *and rise for my help!*
> *Draw the spear and javelin*
>   *against my pursuers!*
> *Say to my soul,*
>   *"I am your salvation!"*
> *Let them be put to shame and dishonor*
>   *who seek after my life!*
> *Let them be turned back and disappointed*

> who devise evil against me!
> Let them be like chaff before the wind,
>   with the angel of the Lord driving them away!
> Let their way be dark and slippery,
>   with the angel of the Lord pursuing them!

And I found Isaiah 49:25 (NKJV):

> But thus says the LORD: "Even the captives of the mighty shall be taken away, And the prey of the terrible be delivered; For I will contend with him who contends with you, and I will save your children."

And Romans 8:31–39 (NKJV):

> What then shall we say to these things? If God is for us, who can be against us? He who did not spare His own Son, but delivered Him up for us all, how shall He not with Him also freely give us all things? Who shall bring a charge against God's elect? It is God who justifies. Who is he who condemns? It is Christ who died, and furthermore is also risen, who is even at the right hand of God, who also makes intercession for us. Who shall separate us from the love of Christ? Shall tribulation, or distress, or persecution, or famine, or nakedness, or peril, or sword? As it is written:

> "For Your sake we are killed all day long;
> We are accounted as sheep for the slaughter."

> Yet in all these things, we are more than conquerors through Him who loved us. For I am persuaded that neither death nor life, nor angels

> *nor principalities nor powers, nor things present nor things to come, nor height nor depth, nor any other created thing, shall be able to separate us from the love of God which is in Christ Jesus our Lord."*

We will fight battles, and let me say that spiritual battles can be messy and violent. We must take heaven by force. Bring heaven down to the place on earth where you need it to rule and reign. Like in UFC, life gets messy, and I find myself praying like a UFC fighter for my family, business, community, and friends. But when I hear that God is our Contender, I know that He will not stop or go into his corner until He conquers all that is in His way to bring us the answers we need to bring us faith, to draw us closer to Him. I understand that He will not stop and has already accomplished the battle at hand, but He allows us to go the distance and know that He carries us, and we do not fight alone.

God cares about what you speak to Him and what is in your heart. He takes your prayers and concerns very seriously and conquers in His time so that the glory goes to Him and Him alone. With leaps and bounds, your faith grows as you watch Him move mountains for you, and He contends for what you contend for, according to His will.

Are you feeling worn out from the battle? Rest in the fact that God is contending for you. He won't stop fighting until the victory is yours.

REFLECT

DAY 25

The Right Tools

They worshipped together at the Temple each day, met in homes for the Lord's Supper, and shared their meals with great joy and generosity

ACTS 2:46

Just as a job becomes easier with the right tools, our spiritual lives require the right tools to grow and fulfill our calling. I want to share something that hit me a couple of weeks ago. We have struggled with our lawn this summer. Well, not the lawn, but the lawnmowers. Yep, you read that right—*lawnmowers*. Plural. We have gone through about five mowers, and the one we currently use is not ours; it is on loan for a few more days. We have had the fast zero-turn mowers and the older, smaller, and much slower mowers. We have pulled mowers out of sheds and rebuilt them. My brother came and cut with his incredible fancy stand-up commercial mower, and now a friend has dropped off a mower as a gesture of kindness. My father, who has been sick and is legally blind, has been our mechanic. It's what he loves to do, so we get the parts, and he makes the repairs, but with him being blind, what takes us five minutes to do can take him hours. Still, we allow him to do what he is good at. It just takes time. (Don't feel sorry for him; he wins at UNO.)

I don't know about you, but the Lord loves to talk when I mow or clean. All summer, I have been making my questions known to the Lord about what to do next with life groups and what groups to be a part of so that I am purposeful in what I am doing for God. I continued to pour out my heart to understand better, and He decided to speak. He said, "Why do you think your friend brought you this lawn mower?" I thought, *well, it's just a nice thing to do.* But He said, "No, he wants a relationship. He needs Me—through you and Ray." The Lord said, "Stop having a Christian life group in your home and invite the lost to a meal in your home. They need a place to belong and to share what is in their heart. No Bible plan, no DVD, just come as you are and sit down and have fellowship." Within a three-mile radius of our home, we have friends and family with whom we are not sharing the gospel and who need a relationship with the Lord.

LYNN THOMPSON

Ray and I have attended several of our lifelong friends' funerals, one only six weeks ago, and we had not shared God with him. The church was standing room only, and more than 75 percent of the people did not know God. They are dying and going to hell. We will continue to watch friends take this same journey as we stand by unless we reconnect—and not to speak Christianese or quote Scripture in a way that believers are comfortable with, but to speak to them with love that they will understand and be available to them right where they are. So, one night a week, we invite enough people to fill up our dinner table, or maybe one at a time, as a small start to build a relationship and have dinner together. This is what God is calling us to do at this time. We are to work this three-mile radius to show the love of God to our neighbors.

In your walk with the Lord, I encourage you to have three things you're always doing: extending a hand to lift up someone, walking side by side with someone, and receiving from a mentor to continue growing.

What spiritual tools are you using? Take stock of the gifts God has given you—prayer, Scripture, fellowship—and put them to use in your daily life.

REFLECT

DAY 26

Representatives of Christ

And whatever you do or say, do it as a representative of the Lord Jesus, giving thanks through him to God the Father.

COLOSSIANS 3:17

As followers of Christ, everything we say and do represents Him to the world. We are His ambassadors, called to reflect His love and truth. This morning, I had a revelation that I hope will resonate with you as it did with me: We get to give back. In prayer time, as we exalt God for who He is and all He has done, I wondered how I could get closer to Him. How can I live a life that honors God?

During my prayer time, I realized something profound: every action I take, no matter how small, is an opportunity to honor God. I must admit that I am so used to living for myself, accomplishing what I have on my plate day in and day out, and thinking, how am I going to get this done? But when the Holy Spirit comes in and brings a revelation, it is as if it is sealed in our hearts, and our understanding is deeper and wider than ever before. Then, we can move with clarity in what that revelation is.

I love the Scriptures, and there have been a handful of times that some verses or passages go deeper in my understanding and manifest than others. Still, this morning, I had one of those moments with Colossians 3:17: "And whatever you do or say, do it as a representative of the Lord Jesus, giving thanks through him to God the Father."

I get to honor God and give back in all I do. Instead of focusing on how I'm going to do what tasks lay before me and thinking how I can't, or how it will be uncomfortable, or even that I should get it over with so I can check it off my list, the Lord gave me a view of what it would look like if I approached each task and gave it back to Him. I would take the focus off myself and focus outward and on Christ.

When we study, honor, and give back to God by committing Scripture to memory, it can be used for its intended purposes. When we work, reflect Christ, and honor God with our work because we are his masterpiece (see Ephesians 2:10), we can achieve what we set out to accomplish. Philippians 1:6 says, "And I am certain that God, who began the good work within you, will continue his work until it is finally finished on the day when Christ Jesus returns."

In our marriages, we honor God by loving our spouse the way God loves us; we love back. Ephesians 5:24–26 (NIV) says, "Now as the church submits to Christ, so also wives should submit to their husbands in everything. Husbands love your wives, just as Christ loved the church and gave Himself up for her to sanctify her, cleansing her by the washing of water through the Word."

When we gather together, we bring Christ with us and overflow with the fruit of the Spirit: love, joy, peace, patience, kindness, goodness, and faithfulness.

How are you representing Christ today? Make it your goal to reflect His love, grace, and truth in every interaction.

REFLECT

DAY 27

God's Will

I know the things you do, and I have opened a door for you that no one can close. You have little strength, yet you obeyed me and did not deny me.

REVELATION 3:8

When God opens a door, it's up to us to walk through it in obedience. Even when we feel weak, His strength enables us to fulfill His will. What do we know about serving God and the kingdom of heaven coming here on earth as it is in heaven?

God has promised to open doors that no one can shut. But we must step through those doors, trusting in His plan, even when uncertain. We know that God is a loving God. We know that He is gracious and merciful. But we also know that God is just. When He speaks, things are accomplished, and no man can tear down what He establishes. What doors He opens, no man can close. What doors He closes, no man can open. When He speaks, creation takes place, and truth and lie must separate. The atmosphere changes by the cutting of His two-edged sword of the Word. What He seals in our hearts is sometimes unspeakable when He is present. We grasp for words that don't measure His presence, but our hearts are sealed like a king's signet ring of His approval.

After reading Hebrews 9 this morning and allowing His presence to teach my Spirit, I want to encourage you today. When helping someone going through an issue or challenging time in life, we often say, "Let's ask that God's will be done." What does that mean? Hebrews 9:16–17 tells us, "In the case of a will, it is necessary to establish the death of the one who made it, because a will does not take effect until the one who made it has died; it cannot be executed while he is still alive." The covenant of forgiveness of our sins could only go into effect once Christ died for our sins. A permanent reconciliation with the Father has always been His will. This is asking for His plan for your life and situation. We think we know the right way if only God would agree with us, but God's plans always draw us to him, which is His Will for us.

In our walk with Christ, it is always His Will that we seek after. Trust His will for your life and know that His ways are greater than our ways. Galatians 2:20 (KJV) says, "I am crucified with Christ: nevertheless, I live; yet not I, but Christ liveth in me: and the life which I now live in the flesh I live by the faith of the Son of God, who loved me, and gave himself for me."

Is there a door God has opened for you? Don't hesitate—step through it in faith, knowing that He will provide everything you need.

REFLECT

DAY 28

Reconciliation

Love prospers when a fault is forgiven, but dwelling on it separates close friends.

PROVERBS 17:9

Reconciliation is restoring relationships—whether between people or between us and God. It is about healing what is broken and making things whole again. On Sundays at church, during altar calls, or just in running into people and talking to them, a question is asked: "How do I forgive someone who has hurt me so much that I can't move on?" Let me be as clear as I can. Forgiveness is more about the person asking how to forgive and the willingness from a changed heart than the person who may have offended us.

Scripture clearly reflects the image and mind of Christ. When we ask for forgiveness, Christ forgives and releases that freedom of unity between us and Him again, and we do not dwell on or constantly relive the wrong. Proverbs 17:9 says, "Love prospers when a fault is forgiven, but dwelling on it separates close friends."

The goal here is reconciliation. Second Corinthians 5:18–19 says, "And all of this is a gift from God, who brought us back to himself through Christ. And God has given us the task of reconciling people to him. For God was in Christ, reconciling the world to himself, no longer counting people's sins against them. And he gave us this wonderful message of reconciliation."

Throughout the Bible, we see stories of reconciliation, from Joseph and his brothers to the ultimate reconciliation through Jesus Christ. God's desire is always to restore relationships. To protect your relationship with Christ and your heart, heed this guidance from Proverbs 23:7 (NKJV): "For as he thinks in his heart, so is he. 'Eat and drink!' he says to you, But his heart is not with you."

True forgiveness has to take place in the heart, or it will separate us from perfect unity with Christ and others, such as friends and family. We may go through the motions of forgiveness, but if we keep it at the forefront of our minds and conversations, we have not forgiven, and our hearts are not close to that person. We don't have to be in the same relationship as before, but we do have to love one another with honest love.

We are beings created in the image of Christ, and to walk in Christ's love, we must guard our hearts. Guarding our hearts means also guarding our tongues because they work together. Proverbs 18:21 tells us, "The tongue can bring death or life; those who love to talk will reap the consequences."

Let's choose words of life from a heart of forgiveness and reconciliation. I encourage you to spend one week speaking life to yourself first and then to those around you and see what changes happen in your life.

Is there a relationship in your life that needs healing? Take a step toward reconciliation today, whether through forgiveness, a conversation, or prayer.

REFLECT

Unnecessary Battles

Not every battle is ours to fight. Sometimes, we waste our energy on unnecessary struggles that distract us from the real battles God has called us to. Unnecessary battles come in many forms—arguments, worries, or situations that don't align with God's plan for us. When we take on these distractions, we lose focus on the battles God has already given us victory over, like standing firm in our faith and protecting our peace. In David's life, we see how he wanted to honor people. He loved honor because God loves honor. David honored the anointing of God on Saul even after God lifted his anointing from him and submitted to that. He honored his relationship with Jonathan by honoring Jonathan's crippled son Mephibosheth. He also wanted to honor Hanun, King Nahash's son, after the king died because of his loyalty.

BEAUTIFULLY ABLE

This is where things take a different turn, though. Hanun was an Ammonite, and the Ammonites were pagan and worshipped other gods. Their hearts were different than the heart of David. David's intention was honor, but the Ammonites' hearts reflected their living situation and their thoughts and reactions to living apart from the one true God.

> *The king of the Ammonites died, and Hanun, his son, reigned in his place. And David said, "I will deal loyally with Hanun, the son of Nahash, as his father dealt loyally with me." So David sent his servants to console him concerning his father. And David's servants came into the land of the Ammonites. But the princes of the Ammonites said to Hanun, their Lord, "Do you think because David has sent comforters to you, that he is honoring your father? Has not David sent his servants to you to search the city, spy it out, and overthrow it?" So Hanun took David's servants and shaved off half the beard of each, cut off their garments in the middle, at their hips, and sent them away.*
>
> *But when the Syrians saw that they had been defeated by Israel, they gathered themselves together. And Hadadezer sent and brought out the Syrians who were beyond the Euphrates. They came to Helam, with Shobach the commander of the army of Hadadezer at their head. And when it was told David, he gathered all Israel together and crossed the Jordan and came to Helam. The Syrians arrayed themselves against David and fought with him. And the Syrians fled before Israel, and David killed of the Syrians the men of 700 chariots, and 40,000 horsemen, and wounded Shobach the commander of their army, so that he died there. And when all the kings who were servants of Hadadezer saw that they had been defeated by Isra-*

el, they made peace with Israel and became subject to them. So the Syrians were afraid to save the Ammonites anymore.

2 SAMUEL 10:1-4, 17-19 ESV

When the Ammonites heard of David's kindness, they didn't believe it. They believed it to be a deceptive and manipulative plan to destroy them and take over the city. They told King Hanun, "Do you really think these men are coming here to honor your father? No! David has sent them to spy out the city so they can come in and conquer it!" King Hanun believed them and retaliated against well-meaning people serving David.

A deceptive heart can not conceive the love, joy, and kindness of God. The Ammonites were dishonest; therefore, they could not believe King David's sincerity and entered a battle that cost many lives. Discernment is key to avoiding unnecessary battles. We need to ask God for wisdom to know when to step in and when to step back. Not every problem is ours to solve, and not every fight requires our involvement. Waste no time with misunderstandings that cost so much. Instead of wasting energy on unnecessary battles, focus on the ones that truly matter. Stand firm in your faith, protect your peace, and obey God's direction. He'll take care of the rest.

Are you fighting battles that aren't yours? Take time to pray and ask God to show you which struggles you need to surrender to Him. Let go of the fights He hasn't called you to, and trust Him to handle the outcome.

REFLECT

DAY 30

Trading Up

And no one puts new wine into old wineskins. For the wine would burst the wineskins, and the wine and the skins would both be lost. New wine calls for new wineskins.

PROVERBS 17:9

Throw off your old sinful nature and your former way of life, which is corrupted by lust and deception. Instead, let the Spirit renew your thoughts and attitudes. Put on your new nature, created to be like God—truly righteous and holy.

EPHESIANS 4:22-24

BEAUTIFULLY ABLE

In life, we're always looking for ways to 'trade up'—whether upgrading our phones, cars, or even homes. But in the kingdom of God, trading up looks different. It's not about material gain but about exchanging our old, broken ways for something far better: God's best. So, here is my truth. Life has been so busy that yesterday I left coffee in the coffee pot on the counter, thinking I would do all my clean up last night, but that didn't happen. This morning, I came into the kitchen and decided to pour a cup of old coffee in a cup and heat it up while I was making another pot. While the coffee was in the microwave heating up, I grabbed the coffee pot to pour the coffee down the sink drains but then realized the dilemma I'd created—to make a fresh pot of new coffee, I needed to pour out the half pot of old coffee first. But what if I needed more coffee before the fresh coffee was made? What if my coffee maker decided to be slow that day?

For a moment, I froze, not wanting to dump out the old coffee. *I might need it before the new coffee is ready.* Then I thought, *Old for new, old for new. This shouldn't be so hard. The new is going to be better coffee. Just let it go.* Then, the thought came to me through conviction, I'm sure. I thought about how many people struggle similarly in their walk with Jesus—holding on to things like unforgiveness, lower self-esteem, or even rejection that causes you to separate from the ones that love you, just holding on just enough that when the first thing goes wrong, you can revert to that familiar place where you have found a false sense of comfort. They are not leaning into the new for fear that it won't work or that there will be too much change, and they will revert to what they come out of. But just like Christ, He is fresh and new every day, not left over, and is more than enough.

God offers us a better deal than anything the world can give. He invites us to trade our fears for His peace, failures for His grace, and weaknesses for His strength. It's the ultimate upgrade and is available to all of us.

Sometimes, we hold on tightly to things that comfort us, even when God offers something better. Trading up means trusting that what God has for us is far greater than anything we hold on to. It's not easy to let go, but we find freedom and fulfillment when we do.

What are you holding onto that God is asking you to trade? Is it fear, doubt, or something else? Today, take a step of faith and 'trade up.' Give God your worries and take His peace. Surrender your plans and receive His purpose.

This is the inner struggle of a coffee addict. Y'all have a fresh cup of coffee and a blessed day.

ADDITIONAL NOTES

www.ingramcontent.com/pod-product-compliance
Lightning Source LLC
Chambersburg PA
CBHW060530080526
44586CB00012B/692